S
TO BE A FIDDLER,
EH BOY?

William Foyle, 1907.
© Hampshire Constabulary History Society.

SO YOU WANT TO BE A PEELER, EH BOY?

The Life and Times of
Sergeant William Foyle
1867–1951

*William Foyle, Ellen Foyle
and John Greenfield*

First published in 2020 by JH Greenfield Family Settlement.
© JH Greenfield Family Settlement, 2020.
www.greenfield-productionsltd.com

🐦 @Oldtimepolicing

First edition published in 2020.

Impressions: 1

A full Cataloguing in Publication record for this book
is available from the British Library.

ISBN: Paperback 9781527266926
ISBN: Hardback 9781527267749

Designed and typeset by Goldust Design
Brand design by Magic Box Media
Printed and bound in the UK by Hobbs the Printers Ltd

For my late father Donald Greenfield

The police are the public and the public are the police; the police being only members of the public who are paid to give full time attention to duties which are incumbent on every citizen in the interests of community welfare and existence.

Sir Robert Peel

CONTENTS

EDITOR'S NOTE

So You Want To Be A Peeler, Eh Boy? is a revelatory account of a patriarch who set out to re-chart his destiny against all the odds. In William Foyle's personal trajectory one can discern a transformation akin to some of the great fictional characters of Charles Dickens, in particular the eponymous David Copperfield and "Pip" Pirrup of *Great Expectations*.

Abject poverty could strike and strike hard in the era in which Dickens wrote his depictions of this social scourge, prevalent at the heart of the nineteenth century's economic powerhouse. His inspiration was first ignited by his Father's spell in Marshalsea Debtors Prison in 1824, secondly, his own experience at the age of 12 of working in a blacking warehouse over-run by rats,[1] and thirdly, by his time as a parliamentary and court journalist proving to be the launch pad for his phenomenal

---

1 One boy Dickens worked with at the blacking factory was called Bob Fagin!

success as a writer and impresario. These three factors also propelled what some biographers and critics have described as his "proto-socialism" – whether accurate or not he was a man determined to expose the dreadful existence of the poor and the hypocrisy of those who were their oppressors.

William too, was propelled by fateful circumstances – in his case that of his mother's death and father's ruination – signalling in turn the prospect of a precarious, meagre existence with few opportunities to rise above his allotted station in life. It is apparent when reading of his youth how the psychological blow of the disintegration of his family was the deep motivational well from which his burning ambition sprang. One could almost imagine if asked for his personal motto it might well have been, "To overcome, to do the right thing, to atone, to restore".

As with most family histories when they come under scrutiny, secrets surface. Illegitimacy, debt, criminality, drunkenness, murder, incest, rape and all manner of misdemeanours are subsequently diluted, re-framed or even wiped entirely from the collective family memory. This happens for a number of reasons such as a sense of family shame, a desire to appear socially respectable, a wish to disassociate from the past, a need to protect, to assume a new identity, or simply because "what's done is done". It's crucial to understand this dynamic when working on and researching family history and this case was no exception. When the primary sources were searched and facts came tumbling forth they began challenging, revising and enhancing the given family account. The result has been the crafting of a far more nuanced survey of William's life and that of his vast, extended kith and kin.

Another feature that comes to the fore in the book is the role of Constabulary wives in supporting husbands in their duties as Policemen. Surprisingly, as detailed, are the range of duties they were expected to perform in addition to raising their families and frequently moving from one post to another. In the case of Ellen, William's spouse, her devotion to this principle is undimmed even through the most heart-rending of circumstances and all the while acting as the ever-present stabilising influence for William and their eight children. Police wives had to be as hardy as their men, which I don't doubt is the same today but with one exception. Women have built careers as Police officers in their own right and they too are likely to have partners who perform the same morale-supporting role as Ellen did for William. The wheels of progress turn.

So You Want To Be A Peeler, Eh Boy? is an intimate portrait of a policing family's experience of living in a community, a country, and a world in constant flux, where they witnessed and played their part in the tumult of two world wars, endured great upheaval, built new lives, gave birth to children, gained new skills and knowledge, and embraced the dividend of post-war opportunities. They may have been "ordinary" people but for sure they lived extraordinary lives.

Dr Susan England

FOREWORD

There are some books whose stories resonate far beyond words on the page. *So You Want To Be A Peeler, Eh Boy?* is one such book. A small book, but one with a unique, real, and personal story bringing to life social history across two centuries, telling of personal determination, renewal in adversity, and the vocation that is being a "Peeler".

Then, as today, policing is the job that touches the widest variety of lives – often at a time of greatest need – in a way really no other does or can. This is a book that highlights a family's commitment to serving, helping, and supporting others. Those who know William Foyle's great-grandson John Greenfield, will also testify to his dedication to this ethos today – continuing an inherent family passion, firmly grafted on the roots put down by the subject of this marvellous book – Police Sergeant (Alfred) William Foyle.

The narrative, originating from the words of William's daughter Ellen Foyle (there is more than one Ellen in this story!) tell of a family love story beset with early deaths, tragedy of losing a farming business, the splitting up of siblings and the underlying determination of addressing these setbacks across generations. It could be said that the experience of losing his mother at an early age, the consequences of such forming the understanding of life that shaped William Foyle's career, and in turn shaped the lives of those who he, as a police officer, husband and father, came into contact over his long life.

There are three strong themes running throughout this excellent book which are both fascinating and speak to us across the years. First, the insight we are given into the life of a police officer at the turn of the nineteenth century and early twentieth which included the expectation that police wives would take an active part in supporting their husband's operational responsibilities, to the extent that an error on her part was a mark against the officer himself.

Secondly, the light it shines on society's reliance then, as now, on an effective, compassionate and flexible police service; on how dependant we are on the individual police officer to maintain safety, uphold the law and prevent offending across the whole community. How then, as now, a local police officer stood for law and order, sending a message of safety and help at hand if needed.

Thirdly, how William Foyle recognised the influence a police officer can have upon the future conduct and life chances of an individual – that punishment is not always the answer to addressing and preventing future offending. In today's language perhaps, he is saying time spent on education, rehabilitation and personal development is most effective in the prevention of future offending; that people deserve a second chance.

From the best of times to the worst of times, a police officer will have to confront the whole gambit of human emotions and reactions of life's rich tapestry – both personal and professional. In this book we follow 84 years of those emotions belonging to William Foyle and his family bridging two centuries, an era of significant social change. However, despite the distance in time, we see the same emotions and reactions experienced by police officers today. William speaks of the challenges of mental health and the importance of talking about the horrors witnessed and of mindful worries. He gives witness to the existence of violence shown to the police and Judges viewing such an offence as a very serious crime, "punishing those guilty without mercy". He recognises the importance of a criminal justice system that protects a Constable in the line of duty with harsh sentences for violence against the police, so that officers know they are "protected by the law". That he feels there were "not sufficient" police officers on the streets is another interesting parallel with challenges facing policing at the time of writing!

Although not described as such, William articulates the need for a stable work life balance and recognises the importance of a happy family environment. This is evidence that pressures on a police officer have not changed much over the decades.

For me, this book really does reach beyond the words on the page. It is not only an insight into social and policing history, but a story that teaches the importance and reward received in giving public service, caring for others, and supporting those who fall on hard times. It tells a love story across the generations of one family and how the support of family and loved ones can inspire and encourage change and happiness out of adversity.

It is a privilege to have been asked by John Greenfield to write the Foreword to this book. I hope everyone who reads it enjoys and learns from its words, as I have done.

Simon Hayes
Ex-Police and Crime Commissioner,
Hampshire Constabulary

PREFACE

What makes a person never give up in the face of challenging circumstances? Is it their determination, their perseverance, a strong belief in what they stand for? I suspect it's a combination of all of those characteristics and more besides.

I often heard from my mother over the years of the man at the heart of this book yet, it was only when I delved into his daughter's written account of her Father's life as a policeman that the sheer enormity of the personal challenge he faced and overcame, made me see him a new light. It had a profound effect on me and as a result I vowed to have his life's story published.

I realised when comparing my life to his in terms of social and economic progression how very fortunate I was to have been born in 1956 and not 1867. How different my early beginnings as a child were when compared to his, which was one of abject poverty and family fragmentation. Nevertheless, we had many things in common: ambition; devotion to family; hatred of social injus-

9

tice, and proud upholders of the laws of this land.

This did not make him – or me – a paragon of virtue. When I was younger rebellion was in my soul perhaps like many in their burgeoning adulthood, which given now I am heavily involved as a volunteer member of the Police family is something I would not have predicted at the time. In the case of William he too, had a streak of non-conformity shown firstly in his late teens when moving away from the county of his birth to look for a brighter future, and then when an officer of two Police Constabularies, by discreetly bending the police rules to help others in dire need.

I began volunteering with the Hampshire Constabulary in 2011, transferring in 2018 to Dorset Constabulary. My volunteering commenced with community speed watching, developing into Police observer roles and way beyond that remit. I have also supported my police volunteering role with a large and engaged social media presence. All of this was my choice, my pleasure, and my passion.

As with great grandfather William, I have witnessed the harm that people do to each other with the result that such experiences leave their mark on mental health and wellbeing. I have held a collapsed and sobbing woman in my arms on being told her son had been murdered; a day in my life I will never forget having seen how another's drug-fuelled actions can destroy a family. This book details the same level of suffering endured by William, which today would be diagnosed as PTSD. Unlike the Victorian era and early twentieth century there is support in place to help police officers through these dark personal struggles.

Policing in William's time was hard and predominantly learnt on the job. If you broke the rules and code of policing you were quickly punished either by wages being deducted, transferal to another Police station, and in more cases than one would think by suspension or dismissal. There were considerable problems also in maintaining police numbers due to the poor quality of some recruits or persistent bad behaviour often involving drunkenness while on duty.

Punishment for those who broke the law was harsh and decisive. Imprisonment for even small offences which sometimes extended to children, widespread corporal punishment, and sentences of hard labour entailing either picking oakum, walking the treadmill, turning a crank in a prisoner's cell, or working in labour gangs.

If William were alive today I think he would be astounded at how society has benefitted from technology, advances in medicine, science and finances, and public service provision. At the same time he might also ponder on why we still see the continued horror of people's disrespect and criminal behaviour on our streets, the growth of cyber-crime, and the pernicious "County Lines" drug gangs preying on young, vulnerable people. Our Police resources in recent years have not grown sufficiently with the times in which we live. Perhaps they never will?

I hope in conclusion that no-one ever loses sight of the fact that whilst Policing is constituted to uphold the laws, serving Police Officers are like most of us. People with families, people who care, professional people, with human frailties, committed to the role they are warranted to uphold. It's not by coincidence that it was written into history by Sir Robert Peel that "The Police are the Public and the Public are the Police".

John Greenfield

SERGEANT WILLIAM FOYLE'S TIMELINE

10 May 1867: Born to John Foyle and Ellen née Dowdell of Fisherton-Delemare, Wiltshire

1879: Mother dies of an abscess of the brain

29th October 1887: Joins Hampshire Constabulary at Winchester Police Station with first posting at Shalfleet, near Newport on the Isle of Wight

15th July 1889: Relocated to Ventnor and promoted to Second Class Police Constable

1890: Isle of Wight became a separate Constabulary under the Local Government Act of 1888

7 May 1891: Marries Ellen Bennett at Stockbridge Parish Church, Hampshire and relocated back to Shalfleet

30th January 1892: A son, Stanley Cecil is born to William and Ellen

Two daughters are born to William and Ellen: Ellen Rosina (1893) and Alice (1896)

1897: A son, William is born to William and Ellen
Posted to Sandown Police Station
Posted to Ventnor Police Station

5th October 1899: Posted to Freshwater

1900: A son, Christopher is born to William and Ellen

1902: A daughter, Ada is born to William and Ellen

1907: A son, Jack is born to William and Ellen

1908: Promoted to Police Sergeant: posted back to Newport

1912: Offered promotion to Inspector

1912: Resigned from Isle of Wight Constabulary

31st January 1913: William, Ellen and the family leave Isle of Wight and relocate to Netley, Southampton

1913: Master of Arms at the new White Star Line based in Southampton Docks

4th August 1914: Great Britain declares war on Germany

1914: Employed as Police Constable at Royal Victoria Military Hospital, Netley

1917: A daughter, Gwendoline Ruth is born to William and Ellen

11th November 1918: Armistice and end of the First World War (The Great War)

1938-39: Leaves Royal Victoria Military Hospital and retires with Ellen to Stockbridge

1st September 1939: Outbreak of Second World War

29th September 1939: Living in Winchester at Market Hall Cottage, Victoria Road (Register of England & Wales 1939)*
Becomes Parish Councillor

20th November 1946: Ellen celebrates 76th birthday

30th November 1947: Ellen dies and is buried at Hound Cemetery, Netley
William moves to Hamble to live with daughter Gwendoline

3rd February 1951: William Foyle dies and is buried at Hound Cemetery, Netley

* The 1939 Register provides a snapshot of the civilian population of England and Wales just after the outbreak of the Second World War. As the 1931 Census for England and Wales was destroyed by fire during the Second World War and no Census was taken in 1941, the Register provides the most complete survey of the population of England and Wales between 1921 and 1951.

Memories of my father. 1867-1951.

On May 10th 1867 there was born to John Foyle and Ellen his wife (née Dowding) a son destined at his birth to become my father. Both his parents were Wiltshire born and at the time of my father's birth at Fisherton-delamere near Devizes were Dairy folk having a dairy and stock which in common with the agricultural folk of that time meant plenty of hard work with no mechanical aids but their two hands so that my father was brought up to know what hard work meant. With the passing of time other children came (he was the eldest) came until there was nine in all. Life went on as life did in those days until my father

Extract from Ellen Foyle's original
"Memories of My Father 1867-1951".
© JH Greenfield Family Settlement.

1

SO YOU WANT TO BE A PEELER, EH BOY?

On 10th May 1867 there was born to John Foyle[1] and Ellen[2] his beloved wife née Dowdell, a son destined to be my Father, Alfred William Foyle. Upon this day three generations of the name Ellen Foyle would feature in our family history.

His parents were Wiltshire-born and at the time of Alfred's birth – later always to be known within the family as William – were dairy folk; hard-working farmers having a large stock producing needy supplies for locals and living in and around Fisherton Delamare and Chitterne, close to Devizes.[3] He was duly educated in the hard work needed to keep the family business going. In those days farming work was mostly under-taken by hand with very little mechanical aids and from a very early age he was taught about the business of working the land and dairy farming.

Andrews' and Dury's Map of Wiltshire, 1810.
© Wiltshire and Swindon History Centre.

Ellen Thompson neé Foyle with daughter
Margaret (later Greenfield), 1938.
© JH Greenfield Family Settlement.

Over the years another seven children were born with my Father being the eldest.[4] Life went on as it did for agricultural workers in those days; toiling hard meant food on the table. At 11 years old he became an apprentice miller. Everything was ground by hand with two stones and when compared to current day practices it's not difficult to imagine how hard and demanding the days were.

Discipline was harsh, no words of encouragement just a firm hand driving a very hard-working group of boys and girls. Father had not long been in his apprenticeship when tragedy struck his Mother to whom he was devoted and whose memory he cherished till his end of days. In 1879, at the age of 33, tired, over-worked, and worn out by chores for her family Ellen died suddenly at home from an abscess of the brain[5] leaving a large family of eight children with the youngest only nine months old.

Tragedy had been bestowed upon them and what had been a family business and a way of life was suddenly gone. Everything that made the home was lost. A broken home is so hard to understand, but sadly it happened to him.

The family eventually separated with Father at just 12 years of age living with his maternal grandmother Thirsa Potter in Fisherton Delamare.[6]

As for his brothers and sisters Caroline moved in with their paternal grandparents Samuel and Elizabeth, and the remaining children – aside from Rosina – were placed in the Warminster Union Workhouse.[7] By 1882 their Father had abandoned them completely.[8]

Father remained with Thirsa until he completed his apprenticeship. As he so often said the work was gruelling for very little reward and he had no desire to remain a miller. He sustained the idea that there had to be something in the world different to farming and milling where little return was seen for such hard labour. His efforts went unnoticed and this played on his young mind. Life for him seemed a destiny already planned and he thought long and hard about what to do. To give so much for very little is a hard lot to accept and being an honourable young man he understood he needed to look further afield. Determined to create a different future for himself he packed his bags and left his grandmother's home and set out for the neighbouring county of Hampshire, which at this time was full of opportunity.

* * *

As his journey began, and even though on occasion he found lodgings and work he often went hungry and cold sleeping rough, and just like

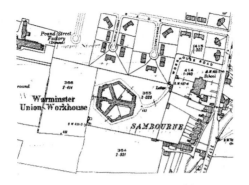

Map layout of Warminster Union Workhouse
© Ordnance Survey.

Facade of the Warminster Union Workhouse.
© Peter Higginbotham.

21

Hampshire Constabulary recruiting poster, 1876.
© Hampshire Constabulary History Society.

Oliver Twist he wanted more. He felt his life had to be transformed into something better and while from a hard-working family background, and an education, he wanted to provide for himself with a safe dwelling and regular food. Onwards he travelled to Winchester where he hoped he may find something that would fulfil his wishes. As he was passing the Police Station at Winchester he spotted a poster calling for recruits:

Hampshire Constabulary want intelligent and active young men, pay on joining nineteen shillings a week, a uniform provided with strong boots. Apply in your own hand writing to the Chief Constable.

He read this several times walking away only to return and read again. It was a cold and bitter snowy day, he was hungry and tired but taking his courage in both hands he walked into the station. He described many times in detail of how the Officer who greeted him was a big burly man with a bristling moustache who looked down at him and after a couple of minutes boomed out loud, "So you want to be a Peeler, eh boy?". Father recalled that as a farmer's boy with rosy cheeks and blue eyes he looked less like a Policeman than anyone in the country.

EXAMINATION
OF A CANDIDATE FOR THE SITUATION OF CONSTABLE.

QUESTIONS	ANSWERS
Name	William Foyle
No.	226
Age	20 ½
Height	5 9
Complexion	Pale
Eyes	Grey
Hair	Black
Particular Marks	None
Where Born — In the Parish of	Netherton Delamere
Where Born — In or near the Town of	Salisbury
Where Born — In the County of	Wilts
Trade or Calling	Labour
Read and Write	Yes
Single or Married	Single
Number of Children	
Last place of Residence	Compton
What Public Service	None
Regiment, Corps, etc.	
Length of Service	
Amount of Pension	
When Discharged	
Do you belong to Army Reserve	
With whom last employed	Mr Pelly
Where last employed	Compton
Have you been Vaccinated	
Do you belong to any Benefit Society	No
Weekly Amount when Sick	

Approved of and Sworn in before us, *William Simonds*

Charles J Fryer

Date 29 Oct 1887

William's "Examination Record of a Candidate for the Situation of Constable", 29th October 1887. It also records his promotion to second Class Police Constable in 1889.
© Hampshire Constabulary History Society.

Yet, as this tale shows his thoughts were misguided. Nerves shaking he was determined to take the steps needed to get a better life. Being very honest he told the officer all the reasons why he wanted to become a Police Constable explaining in detail his background, his passion to help others and how he needed to find a role that provided for him and his life ahead.

The Officer in charge turned out to be a "good sort" who sat him down and told him all about what it meant to be a Police Constable in the late 1880s. He explained how it worked, what you may see, the good, the bad and the terrible, and the sad things that people do. He also explained in detail the possible effect the duties of a policeman may have upon your life. This never changed Father's mind at all, he wanted to try.

It appeared fate had played a hand as that year Hampshire Constabulary had put recruiting posters up on most street walls around the county. Everything was working in his favour and on 29th October 1887 he was accepted and joined the Constabulary with the collar number of 226 at the age of 20. His first posting was at Shalfleet Police Station on the north-west of the Isle of Wight. A proud first step in what would be a life's journey protecting others and upholding the laws of our great land. Nervous but determined he went into the station on his first day and stepped towards an incredible life in the service to others.

During his training as a recruit he often wondered how he would measure up but as was the case throughout his life he let nothing beat him. He had this attitude if it lay within his power he would do it to his best ability no matter what it took. Training was hard with very long days, many sleepless nights but he stood tall and was resolute in his wish to become a good Police Constable. The training was very basic in those days, hard discipline, rules you must abide by, and being taught how to enforce the laws of the time. To learn what was required seemed a daunting task at times and some he faced were dark days. He often said he had to think positively for he knew the challenge was going to be a tough one

Some months had passed and he was doing well; hard lessons taught and learnt and being shown things that distressed him. Apart from his Mother he had never seen a person who had died. This he found hard at first but he came to understand that it was part of Police life to see and deal with tragedy. Notwithstanding, he was resolute in his mind that this was for him. The Constable's role had many demands for you had to be strong yet fair. You needed to undertake tasks that would shock you, to break awful news to families, but do this with compassion.

Without much further training under his belt he was left to learn as he went along. In those days a person's character and views, their courage in the face of traumatic events and scenes played a huge part in how you policed. Policemen were known as "Bobbies" or "Peelers", the latter after Sir Robert Peel.[9] The uniform they wore was smart and included a dark blue long coat and a

Sir Robert Peel (1788-1850), portrait by George Raphael Ward.
© Scottish National Portrait Gallery.

tall hat. They were unarmed except for a heavy wooden truncheon. The idea was to make Police Constables as unlike the army as possible but this left many open to attacks from criminals who had no fear of the laws or the consequences. Every day he learned more and more and it was a hard learning curve. If you made a mistake and it fell before your senior officers you would be punished. Harsh learning and hard lessons were taught – Father often told me of this.

A "Peeler" of the Metropolitan Police c. 1850s.
© Metropolitan Police Museum.

His life on the Isle of Wight was fairly uneventful to begin with, however that would soon change as he became more active on his beat. There were a few cases of sheep rustling, drunken soldiers, and bad behaviour; a Policeman then was expected to deal with many incidents and encounters by himself. He could cuff an ear and give a stern lecture to make his point known. People accepted that your Constable was the one you listened to and the one you sought advice from if matters were troubling you. Father's duty was to uphold the laws of our land with Police work that involved walking many miles every day whilst proudly treading the beat.

As the streets were cobbled and hard on the legs and feet good boots were a must, always polished and shiny. Constables were inspected daily by their Sergeant before going out on the beat as they were deemed pillars of the community.[10] Uniforms had to be clean and smart before venturing on to the streets, an image of authority that the public could see.

Pedal cycles were available but Father always said he could do better on foot. Very tiring days for him but he loved his job. Often a Police Constable was moved around from one place to another sometimes as a punishment or in other cases by what local people needed. As was the normal drill he too was required at a different location on the Island and subsequently relocated from Shalfleet to Ventnor on 5th July 1889. In the case of a town Police Constables only moved from one division to another and he welcomed the change. After having now served for two years and taken many cases before the Police courts he had established an understanding that his lot was a happy one. I could list many incidents during those early years but instead I will tell of just some he dealt with; some will be sad, some will be of historical interest but above all this was his experience of policing.

At this time there were about 60,000 Police Officers on the streets in England which was generally agreed not sufficient and often questioned. They worked long hours, often day-after-day with no breaks. The driving passion was to do what was right. I recall seeing him come home after a long, tiring day, fall into his chair with his head in hands sobbing at what he had witnessed. Yet, this was what he wanted to do with a burning desire. His Police life was shortly to experience a big change for his destiny was written. I am going back to before I was born to recall the next part of his story, which he told me about with true love and deep emotion.

* * *

His life here was fairly uneventful, and as is usual in County Police forces he was transferred from Cowes to Ventnor. (In a town constabulary they only move from one division to another all in the same town) and welcomed the change. He had now been in the force three years and had had many cases in the Police Courts so that was now well established as a policeman and finding that after all his was a happy life. While at Ventnor he met Ellen the fifth daughter of Mr and Mrs James Bennet of Stockbridge, Hampshire and on May 9th [they were married at]

Extract from Ellen Foyle's original
"Memories of My Father 1867-1951".
© *JH Greenfield Family Settlement.*

31

While serving at Ventnor he met Ellen, the fifth daughter of Mr and Mrs James Bennett of Stockbridge, Hampshire. He had fallen in love with the wonderful woman who became my Mother. After a courtship and permission from her Father and his station Inspector[11] they married on 7th May 1891 at Stockbridge Parish church.[12] They subsequently relocated back to the little village of Shalfleet, near Newport where they moved into their first married station and commenced a very happy, eventful married life of 56 years.

Shortly before their marriage the Isle of Wight became a separate Police Force in April 1890: the Isle of Wight Constabulary. Nonetheless, and as far as my Father was concerned, it was still his beloved Hampshire Constabulary. In keeping with the rules all officers were given the opportunity to join it or relocate back to the mainland. He decided the Island life was for him and stayed put and within a year their first child and son, Stanley Cecil, was born unto them on 30th January 1892.

Notes

1 John was the son of Samuel Foyle (1819-1884) and Elizabeth Mead née Ingram (b.1812) and subsequently baptised on 4th February 1849 in Chitterne (Parish Records; CSM Baptisms). According to the 1861 Census he was a plough boy. He is also recorded in the Agricultural Labour Census of 1871.

2 Ellen was born on 4th April 1844 at South Newton, near Salisbury, the illegitimate daughter of Thirsa Dowdell. Thirsa married Ellen's presumed father, John Potter in 1847 and they produced a large family. John was a Royal Marine from 1836 to 1846 and fought for a short period in the Maori Wars that waged from 1845 to 1872 in New Zealand. See Maori Wars (New Zealand Wars) at https://en.wikipedia.org/wiki/New_Zealand_Wars

3 According to the England & Wales Census of 1871 the family were living at 2 Bidden Lane in Chitterne St Mary, Wiltshire. By the England & Wales Census of 1911 Alfred is now registered as William Foyle and is living at Lukely Cottage, Mill Street, Newport (on the Isle of Wight) with his wife and six children: Ellen Rosina (b.1893), Alice (b. 1896), William (b.1897), Christopher (b.1900), Ada (b.1902), and Jack (b.1907). Other official records show two other children bringing the total by 1917 to eight: Stanley Cecil (1892-1968) and Gwendoline Ruth (1917-1971).

4 William's siblings were Rosina Ellen (1869-1935), Caroline Annie (1871-1952), Ellen Frances (1872-n.d.), Stanley George Foyle (1874-1923), Louisa Emma (1875-1951), Lucy Mary (1877-1901), and Thomas Leonard Foyle (1878-1931).

5 As documented in the record of her death in the "December quarter" in the Warminster district.

6 England & Wales Census 1881 which was taken on 3rd-4th April.

7 See http://www.workhouses.org.uk/Warminster/#Records

8 Based on the research undertaken by Roger Foyle, John Foyle had a price on his head by 1882 and was wanted by the police. See http://www.chitterne.com/history/

9 Whilst today's police officers are known colloquially as "Bobbies" they were once more commonly known as "Peelers" deriving from Lord Robert Peel, the founder of the first professional police force: the Metropolitan Police. Subsequent police constabularies were based on this model. The first 1,000 of Peel's police, who wore uniforms of blue tail-coats and top hats, began patrolling the streets of London on 29th September 1829. The uniform was carefully chosen to ensure "Peelers" look more like ordinary citizens than a red-coated soldier with a helmet. See https://www.historic-uk.com/HistoryUK/HistoryofEngland/Sir-Robert-Peel/ and https://en.wikipedia.org/wiki/Robert_Peel

10 Discipline was harsh for Policemen at this time and this extended to their wives. Before the age of telecommunication Police officers were very much left to their own devices when on the beat, however there was a strict daily requirement of "making points", which entailed meeting their Sergeant at a set time at a set location. Failure to meet points could result in fines and if persistent, dismissal. Drunkenness on duty was a frequent occurrence as was receiving "treats" (gifts in kind). Examples of indiscipline taken from Hampshire and Isle of Wight police officers' records cover a variety of transgressions, for example: "Charles KNIGHT 158, 8th March 1872, Associating and drinking with a member of a family of thieves on the 4th inst, for having been drunk and conveyed in a helpless state to the Police Station at Totton. Fined a week's

pay and returned to the second class"; "William George
MILLS 21, 1st December 1905, Having between the 23rd
and 30th Sept 1905 been guilty of conduct likely to bring
discredit upon the force by taking an old cloth from a clothes
line to wipe his boots with and then throwing it away. Fined
one week's pay"; and "George FULLER 140, 23rd Feb 1891,
Called on to resign as useless". See *Policing Hampshire and the
Isle of Wight: A Photographic History*, Lee, John, Peake, Colin,
Stevens, Derek and Williams, (Clifford, Phillimore & Co.
Ltd), 2001, pp. 2-4.

11 Apparently, and up until the late 1980s, not only did
officers have to ask permission for where they could reside but
also whether they could get married. In addition the behaviour
of spouses could be held against an officer. Ibid, *Policing
Hampshire and the Isle of Wight: A Photographic History*, p.2.

12 England & Wales Marriage Index 1837-2000. Stockbridge
has a twelfth century chapel now known as St Peters, which
was served by the "head-minster" at King's Somborne as were
other chapels in the "Hundred". Thus, although Stockbridge
became a flourishing small borough, which eventually gained
parliamentary representation, it never had a parish church of
its own until 1848.

*Hampshire Constabulary officers who transferred to the
Isle of Wight Constabulary on 31 March 1890.
William is in the back row, third left.
© Hampshire Constabulary History Society.*

2

THREE LIVES: YARMOUTH, FAMILY, AND POLICING

Not long after the birth of my brother Father was relocated once again, this time back to Yarmouth Police station. He was now entitled to quarters known as a Police house attached to the station. The house was comfortable with an open coal fire and three rooms with a scullery. A garden of small size was somewhere we could play. During his service here he and Mother had two daughters, myself named after her, and my sister Alice.

Continuing to prove to be a very good Police Constable he sustained his record of bringing many cases before the courts. He often felt sad at some he presented as they were often hungry, homeless, and stole to survive. A Policeman's lot can be difficult but decisions were based on a clear what's right and what's wrong. It fell upon my Mother to search all the female prisoners brought to the cells attached to the station.

If the Policeman was married it was his wife's obligation to assist him in his service. Mother was a good wife and stood beside him and did all she could to help him in his duty. Thus, he would give her a list of her tasks to fulfil. This service whilst voluntary was considered a wife's paramount duty with no exceptions.

In the age when he was writing his diaries prisoners did not receive any comforts and the cells were very basic with stone beds. Cold, dark and scary, an unpleasant place to be confined, they too were a form of punishment. It was the Police Constable's duty to ensure that the rules of arrest were carried out whether male or female and there was a "no compassion rule"; the law had been broken and you must be punished.

Times were hard and in most cases very little sympathy was shown for criminals. Justice was harsh, sentences were often hard labour, and we had the birch too. The birch was a terrible way of beating a person – a big mass of sticks that inflicted terrible pain. On one occasion I remember Mother telling me of a case whereby a young girl had been arrested for stealing a brooch. She was bought into the cold cell on a winter's night and searched. The brooch was found and

The River Yar (Yarmouth on the left, Norton on the right).
Engraved by George Bannon, 1831.

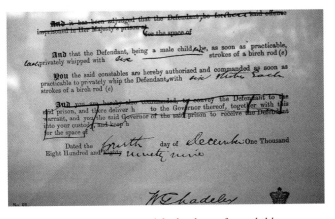

A Magistrate's committal for birching of two children,
4th December 1899.
©West Midlands Police Museum.

she remained under arrest. While being questioned she said she had found the brooch and not stolen it.

On being questioned a second time it transpired she was a well-educated girl who had fallen upon hard times and been in bad company. The cells for women and men were the same, a hard cold stone bed, no pillow and only a thin blanket to cover. The girl was shaking with the cold and tearful and Mother was quite saddened by this and being compassionate took her a pillow from our home. It was common practice for the policeman's wife to hold the keys to the station while the Police Constables were out on the beat. She had hoped that before Father returned in the morning she would be able to remove the pillow and no-one would know of her weakness. Unfortunately, the Sargeant had dropped into the cells with another prisoner and saw the pillow. Upon returning to the station Father was held responsible for her kindness, which was considered an offence, and was duly fined a week's pay. The Inspector who issued the fine warned him most vigorously that any further action of this kind would not be tolerated. Fines were inflicted on Police Officers if they failed to adhere to the rules. Mother often said this was the first and last time she let her heart rule her head as in actual fact her actions could have meant instant dismissal for her husband. She apologised to Father and his Sergeant but the rules had been broken, the guilty, no matter who must be punished. My parents learnt a valuable lesson in Police life.

Those in charge always wanted Police Constables to work with a positive mind of commitment but also believed they should appreciate their job security and the welfare schemes offered by being in the Constabulary. There were strict rules with no exceptions, loss of pay and loss of pension to try to stop those unhappy leaving. The very same privileges or rather the prospect of losing them, was intended to serve as a deterrent to breaking the rules or thinking of leaving without good cause. I think Father was contributing two shillings a month to his pension at this point in time, which was a huge amount to lose if things went wrong.

His stay at Yarmouth was not very eventful and was very much as a policeman's life was expected to be. There were one or two sad cases but in general daily life was quite good. Finding poor souls who had passed away at home was always difficult and when he found someone who was living a sad life, dead, it affected him. So many had very little and lived in terrible conditions but it motivated him and drove him to work harder to make changes to help others more. When a child dies, one whose life has many years ahead, it is terribly hard to understand. In his career he saw many dead children and he always felt that no matter what he came upon and its circumstances, he would deal with it as best he could. If it was someone's fault he would use the laws to bring those responsible to court. I recall in one conversation how he told us about respecting the law and those who devoted their life to enforcing said laws. Father was an upstanding man and did all he could to bring pride to the uniform he wore.

* * *

The locals who lived around us were generally very peaceful. We had the normal drunken fisticuffs and some local theft but Yarmouth in those days was not very different to that of today. They were a pleasant community with a travelling population, yachts, and passengers on steamers bringing much life to the town. Socially there were some divides as not everyone had money.

The local councils in those days followed tradition and managed the towns wisely. Whilst the rules were strict and sometimes deemed unfair to people, what was essential was for everyone to feel and be safe in their homes. The known fact was that on many days you would see Constables on the beat with the result that local people got to know their local Bobby. Above all they knew he stood for law and order. This sent a message of safety for they knew that help was there if needed. Community spirit was in everyone's hearts at that time and the more they worked together the less crime became their focus. The Constabulary's stance was that if the public and Police were seen to work in tandem it would bring peace. Even those who fell afoul of the law learned a lesson that it is far better to be law-abiding than do hard time.

No one had much and we would often see people sharing food and old clothing, the simple

The River Yar (Yarmouth on the left, Norton on the right). Engraved by George Bannon, 1831.

things that helped another. Again I quote Father: "If you help your fellow man and you do what is right, your actions will bring rewards much greater than money." I often wondered what he meant at the time but now I know. If you do good things for others you feel good; it's a lesson for all.

One of the traditions in our town where all the community came together was on 5th November for Guy Fawkes celebrations, with a huge bonfire built on waste ground and a big fireworks display. On one such occasion the local postman was tasked with the role of commentator. As he stepped forward to address the crowd, the bonfire structure which was blazing, collapsed upon him. Father was tasked with removing the debris and the postman's body. I cannot bring myself to write the words he said of what he had to do that night. The images remained with him for many years. But I do remember he said the poor man's wife was present at the time and witnessed this awful tragedy. As I write these words my eyes fill with tears for I can still hear him telling Mother of his task on that dreadful night. From that day onward until 1952, the tradition of celebrating 5th November in the town was stopped.

This was only one of many incidents in his four years at Yarmouth. He often said to us, "It's hard to believe that people do the things they do to each other, the unkindness and hurt they place on each other at times is awful to find." A Policeman has to understand death, has to come to terms with incidents many people will never witness or experience. The awful sight of injuries and terrible acts of violence inflicted upon others. This can, and I know it did, hurt Father and affected his emotions. His belief was that if you feel sorrow for what you see this allows you to deal with it easier. I never quite understood what he meant but as I grew older I realised that to be a Policeman you had to be tough but keep fellow feeling and understanding close to your heart.

There were a number of months where we had a welter of bad crimes in Yarmouth because of some very bad people who had located to the Island. There were deaths, men and women, terrible beatings and thefts but Father did his best. It then became a problem in Sandown with thefts and other terrible occurrences and so he was again relocated.[1] From the very day we arrived at our new Police house Father was extremely busy; a lot of duties with very little time off. It fell upon his lot to work seven days for many months with only an hour on Sunday to go to church. Some days his work would have to continue into the night. I can see him in my mind coming home dropping into a chair, lowering his head and sobbing into his hands when he had seen death close up. These images stay lodged in your mind and I remember him saying that until you bring those images out and explain them to others you will still feel the pain. He often said if he talked to Mother and other Constables he felt the worry decline. She would cradle him in her arms telling him all would be well, it was his job and not any fault of his. I know she shared many tears with him, holding hands in front of the coal fire talking and sharing the sorrow – it's not the side of policing many ever see.

But he cared about people in a way that is hard to explain. Nothing was too much trouble, going far beyond the Policeman's duty to be kind. I hope, if in years to come and should Constables carry the same fears from what they witness

Sandown, c.1920s.
© UK Photo and Social History Archive.

46

they will talk to family and friends. The mind is a camera and from it an album of pictures is formed and it should be shared.

Life became even busier in Sandown. Mother was tasked with not only her Police custody duties but looking after her family and sadly her health failed rapidly. She became tired and unable to keep going. Father, while deeply and passionately committed to his duty, asked for another station where hopefully duties would be a little lighter. To his delight and given the circumstances the Constabulary agreed to his request and we moved back to Ventnor where thankfully her health improved. It took time but he did all he could between his duty and home life to get her well again. He confided in me that his heart was broken that Mother had become ill as a result of his work.

Notes

1 "TRANSFER...PC FOYLE who has been stationed here at Yarmouth for some time, has this week been removed to Sandown and the best wishes of the inhabitants go with him for his future success and promotion in the force". *Isle of Wight County Press*, 17th October 1896. See http://www.annbarrett. co.uk/police/police-snippets-from-old-newspapers/

A New and Corrected Map of the Isle of Wight and Outline of the Southern Coast of England. Engraved by George Bannon, 1831.

3

VENTNOR, FRESHWATER, AND THE NATURE OF CRIME ON THE ISLAND

As always it was busy for Father although he was able to deal with most incidents that came his way but around this time there were outbreaks of sheep maiming at Freshwater and he was sent there on special duties to uncover those behind this terrible act. Why and who would do these terrible things to animals was very concerning. A vile act of abuse, and in some cases very disturbing incidents came to light. Needless to say several men were caught and imprisoned for many years for acts of perversion.

Having identified and caught those responsible Father became very popular with the locals and they called upon the powers-that-be to make him their Constable. It was agreed and on 5th October 1899 we moved to Freshwater. Once more we set up home. Adjoined to the Police station it was comfortable, we had food, warmth and here we spent some very eventful years. The house was large with a huge open fire grate, a garden and scullery. The sleeping rooms were small but comfortable. Police life was indeed giving us what our Father, a man of humble background had dreamt of as a young man.

The list of cases he dealt with would be too long to list as they ranged from theft, assault, murder, accidents, shootings and knife crimes and all hard to face. Unbelievably he showed no fear, he was not afraid to confront anyone. He also had duties that saw him helping out at major occasions which dictated smart dress uniform. I remember

Ventnor from the pier, 1899.

one was the sad death of our Queen Victoria on
22nd January 1901 when he had to help oversee
the moving of Her Majesty from Osborne House
via Cowes to the mainland. He remembered in
exact detail the whole scene; Cowes was then a
popular resort and its regatta world famous. He
described standing to attention saluting Her
Majesty's coffin as it passed. There was a proces-
sion of Horse Guards moving along the street in
Cowes watched by other Guards and spectators
of all ages. Police Officers marched followed by
more Guards with big drums and a huge military band. He said Queen Victoria's coffin was

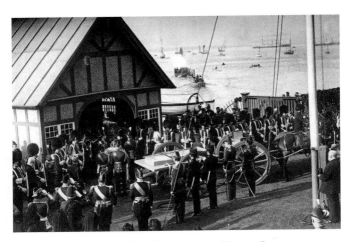

Queen Victoria's coffin arriving at Trinity Quay,
Cowes, for transfer to the mainland.

on a gun carriage pulled by horses and even more officers and Guards followed on foot. The Royal Yacht *HMY Victoria and Albert* anchored off Cowes harbour was a splendid big yacht, grandeur beyond our dreams. He described the hundreds of people gathered that day, the weeping and tears that flowed, how emotional he felt and what an honour it was to be present.

Father met many foreign Royal dignitaries in his career amongst them the late Kaiser Wilhelm II[1] and King Alfonso VIII of Spain.[2] He was also present at events where King Edward VII attended. He was on duty for Princess Beatrice[3] many times when she was in attendance on the Island in her official role as Governor and he had many anecdotes about his duties, such as being on guard duty for 12 hours outside, no matter what the weather. Nevertheless, it was considered an honour to be tasked to guard Royalty and another duty he was very humbled by.

Another case I want to share is when he was called upon to deal with a young boy caught stealing fruit, a simple theft of some old apples. In those days a Constable's job was to deal with these things by a simple leather glove round the ear and a harsh lecture to be followed by taking the child back to parents and telling them about the incident and how punishment had been given.

*Princess Beatrice of
Saxe-Coburg.
© Royal Collection.*

*Pearl Craigie, 1902.
Photographer,
George Charles Beresford.*

In this instance he found a family living in terrible conditions with little food, a cold house and no money for coal. He was so sad he thought he should help. With this in mind he went back to our home, found some food and even took a sack of coal to the family. Of this unfortunate affair he remarked, "I may be a Police Constable and it's my duty is to keep the peace and uphold the law, but that does not stop me being a human being who cares."

Life in the early 1900s was not easy, many had very little while the fortunate had so much. As a hard-working Police Constable he had a regular wage, we had food and warmth as a result of his work. We lived a simple life, one that saw us as a family going to church each Sunday to give thanks for what we had. In our world and in our lives we must appreciate every blessing we have.

There were many famous people who spent time on our beloved Isle of Wight and also lived here at various points. For example, Sir Edward Elgar, a renowned composer of many fine pieces of music, also Mahatma Gandhi was rumoured to have stayed close to Osborne House, home of our Queen Victoria.[4] We also had some famous people die while on the Island. One in particular was the author Pearl Craigie[5] who wrote under the *nom de plume* of John Oliver Hobbes and lived in St Lawrence Lodge in Ventnor. Sadly she died in her sleep in 1906 at the young age of 39.

Our beloved Isle of Wight was a wonderful place to live and many who visited during our time liked it a great deal because there was so much to see and people travelled from long distances to enjoy the beautiful views, the beaches, and the marvellous countryside. Father would tell us of the many times he spent chatting to visitors and describing his life in the Constabulary, always speaking highly of his job and explaining that a Police Constable's life can be both sad and happy.

As mentioned earlier, we were taught the cardinal rule of respecting the laws and those charged with upholding them. Our behaviour could affect our Father's job; he was the driving force behind our lives and because of him, his hard work and dedication to his duties, we were happy. There was an incident one summer's evening when he was attacked for stopping two men stealing from a farmer's field. Both men young in years, took it upon themselves to punch and kick him in an attempt to escape. They inflicted a cut eye and bruises to his face and body. Fortunately being a big man and strong his attackers swiftly regretted their actions. The truncheon is a formidable weapon if used properly, and drawing his, he subdued both men who sustained injured limbs and badly cut faces.

Calling for assistance by shouting and blowing his whistle another Constable close by heard his calls for help. When he reached Father the two men were taken to the prison cell at Ventnor Police station. I am not sure what happened to them after their time in prison but I do remember both received three years hard labour. This was in the days when if you attacked a Constable the judges viewed this is a very serious crime punishing those guilty without mercy. I thought the punishment given the two men was very harsh but Father soon corrected my misguided view. He said: "Ellen, I am a Police Constable. My job is to uphold the laws of our great country, if in doing this I am injured in the execution of my duty then I look to the judges to protect me and show we will not accept this action. When those who hurt us are found guilty we Constables know our judges will be tough."

Once more another valuable lesson was learnt. I hope in years to come the same views are upheld. It's important that Police Constables know they are protected in law.

Notes

1 Wilhelm II or William II (*Friedrich Wilhelm Viktor Albert*); 1859-1941) was the last German Emperor (*Kaiser*) and King of Prussia. He reigned from 1888 until his abdication on 9th November 1918 shortly before Germany's defeat in the First World War.

2 Alfonso XIII (1886-1941), also known as "El Africano" or sometimes "The African", was King of Spain from 1886 until the proclamation of the Second Republic in 1931. Alfonso was monarch from birth as his father, Alfonso XII, had died the previous year. Alfonso's mother, Maria Christina of Austria, served as Regent until he assumed full powers on his 16th birthday in 1902.

3 Princess Beatrice, the youngest of Queen Victoria's nine children was Governor of the Isle of Wight from 1896 until

her death in 1944. She was also President of the Frank James
Memorial Hospital at East Cowes from 1903 until her death.

4 For more about the famous personages who visited and
stayed in Ventnor, including George Bernard Shaw and Karl
Marx, and where Charles Dickens wrote six chapters of *David
Copperfield* see http://www.ventnortowncouncil.org.uk/about-
famous.php

5 Pearl Mary Teresa Craigie (1867-1906) was an Anglo-
American novelist and dramatist who wrote under the name
of John Oliver Hobbes. Though her work fell out of print
in the twentieth-century, her first book *Some Emotions and
a Moral* published in 1891 was a sensation in its day, selling
80,000 copies in only a few weeks. From 1900, she lived and
worked at her villa near her parents' home at St Lawrence, Isle
of Wight. The villa is now called Craigie Lodge and bears a
small commemorative plaque memorializing her time there.
She was President of the Society of Women Journalists in
1895 and also a member of the Anti-Suffrage League. The
University of Reading holds a collection of Craigie's papers
comprising letters written by her from 1898-1905 to Bishop
W.F. Brown, who at the time was a Roman Catholic priest in
charge of a "slum" parish in South London, and two scrap-
books, one relating to an American visit 1905-1906 and the
other containing cuttings about her death and funeral in 1906.
See https://www.reading.ac.uk/special-collections/collections/
sc-craigie.aspx

*Marconi's Transmitter at Knowles Farm, Niton, adjacent
to St Catherine's Point Lighthouse, Isle of Wight.
© Isle of Wight History Society.*

4

MARCONI, SHIPPING DISASTERS AND BEER

I think one of Father's proudest moments in a long Police career was on 12th December 1901 when he was called to duty at a small hut at Knowles Farm in Niton, close to St. Catherine's Point Lighthouse.[1] Adjacent to the Atlantic the hut proved to be a fitting venue for what became a momentous occasion. His task was to stand guard outside on a freezing cold day while the first successful wireless signal to cross the Atlantic was sent by John Barron from Poldu on the Lizard Peninsula in Cornwall to the inventor Guglielmo Marconi[2] at St. John's in Newfoundland.[3] Unbeknown to many at the time Father was invited inside the hut where he recalled seeing a little black box around which a group of people were talking excitedly whilst waiting to hear whether the signal had been successful. Being the only Police Constable on duty it's not hard to imagine his excitement and pride on realising that he had played a quiet part in bringing the world to our Island doorstep. I found it strange that it was not big news at the time given the significant advances this made to all. It may have been because there was very little way of spreading news, whether good or bad – it was generally done by mouth. I wondered why he was not mentioned as being present but as he said, "I was just doing my job Ellen, no more, no less".

There are many accounts of how Marconi's invention of radio transmission saved lives and two come to mind. The first is of the French aviator and inventor Louis Blériot,[4] who was the first to fly an aircraft across the English Channel on 25th July 1909 carrying onboard a radio transmitter box. The second is my recall of Father mentioning that during the *Titanic* disaster in 1912 many lives were saved by Marconi's wireless telegraphy.[5]

We had some very sad incidents within the waters that surrounded our great Island. I can remember two that were very bad. A military ship just off St Catherine's point was hit by another ship, I believe it was called *HMS Tiger*[6] and the latter was badly damaged and split in two. The bow sank quickly but the stern stayed afloat for a short while. A few sailors were saved that night but sadly we learned 27 souls lost their lives. A

Guglielmo Marconi, 1908.
© Library of Congress Prints and Photographs Division,
Washington, D.C. USA.

Guglielmo Marconi with instruments used to
receive first transatlantic message at St. John's,
Newfoundland, 12th December 1901.
Photographer James Vey.
© NewFoundland Provincial Archives.

HMS Tiger tribute postcard, 1908.
http://www.olioweb.me.uk/echoes/?page_id=240

Lieutenant Middleton and the crew of HMS Tiger.
https://undereveryleaf.wordpress.com/2017/09/17/
the-h-m-s-tiger-disaster-2nd-april-1908/

similar terrible disaster happened on a cold day in 1908 with snows falling the ship *HMS Gladiator* hit the *SS St Paul* with many lost lives again, over 25 if I remember correctly.[7]

* * *

You never knew what each day would bring and what Father might have to deal with. One particular case was something of a mystery to unfold. A large number of 25 gallon casks of beer disappeared from the Freshwater hotel store shed, and presumed stolen. It was a mystery. However, there were a lot of militia men stationed nearby and investigations found no evidence, or the casks, but the condition of some of the men raised suspicion. More enquires were made by Father at the Golden Hill Fort[8] but to no avail.

Being one who followed his instinct he decided to watch from a location close-by at night, and on his first attempt spotted what had transpired. The casks had been removed and buried in the ground at the bottom of the cliffs for the men to return to at any time. They were caught out as three men spotted by Father had approached him rather drunkenly asking for directions back to the Fort. Using his whistle to call for help several arrests were made. Apparently each night at lights out they would wander down to the casks, fill their tankards and return to the Fort having drunk all they wanted.

Needless to say they were charged with theft and being soldiers and persons of trust dealt with accordingly. Theft was not accepted lightly no matter the perpetrator and the judges passed very harsh sentences. Whilst the case had been resolved and the sentences passed a mystery still remained. The casks were large, heavy, and hard to move and at that time there were no motor vehicles so how did they move the casks a few miles and get them to bottom of the cliffs? The answer was never found.

There are so many stories of incidents that happened in those days, for example there was a series of robberies at a large private home owned by Colonel Derby, an artillery Officer. A lot of money, hundreds of pounds was stolen over a period of time and Father was given the task of finding out who was responsible and how it was happening. After extensive enquires over several months he identified various soldiers staying at the property, with some returning. It was this rotation that matched to the times of each of the thefts from Colonel Derby. Eventually he discovered that three soldiers had been living well above the normal standards for the time and it was because of this they were questioned about the thefts. The youngest was just 18 years

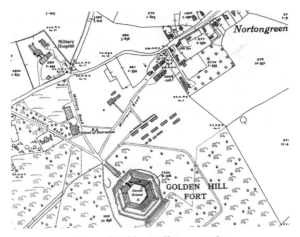

Map of Golden Hill Fort. 1862.
© Ordnance Survey.

Freshwater Bay. Engraved by George Bannon, 1831

old. He broke down and confessed to being one of the thieves. All three were sentenced to long terms in prison and Father was commended for his hard work in bringing this case before the judges.

Through his vigilance and commitment to duty many other cases were brought to the courts. I write my diaries and memories with such pride because he was an outstanding Police Constable and thrived on being part of Hampshire and Isle of Wight Constabularies. He was very popular with the residents of Freshwater and even those he had put "inside" never gave him any trouble. What was so wonderful is that the locals looked upon him as a friend, someone they could turn to in time of need, and the juvenile population came to understand discipline and respect even when the catapult or an apple tree was temptation because Father's big burly Policeman's clip around the ear made them think twice. His hard work and logical devotion brought much peace to the local villages.

Notes

1 Telegraphy – sending electronic messages along metal wires – was first theorized by the seventeenth century scientist, architect and polymath Robert Hooke; it was only after the start of the Industrial Revolution that it became practically possible. Marconi set up the Niton transmitter in 1900 having dismantled his first transmitter at The Needles near Alum Bay. The last transmission from The Needles was made on 26th May 1900. Working at Niton Marconi successfully designed the first selectively tuned wavelength effectively avoiding interference. Orders for ship radio now started to pour in. Marconi invested another £50,000 into two new radio stations at the Lizard Peninsula in Cornwall, in the USA, and Canada for the next great breakthrough of transmitting across the Atlantic. On 23rd January 1901 the Knowles Farm station transmitted radio waves that were picked up 299 kilometres away at the new station in Cornwall, twice the distance of any previously recorded radio transmission. This proved the long-held scientific theory that radio waves would follow the curvature of the Earth. See Medland, John, "The Isle of Wight and the Birth of Radio", *Newport Beacon*, December 2007.

2 Guglielmo Marconi, 1st Marquis of Marconi FRSA (1874-1937) was an Italian inventor, and electrical engineer known for his pioneering work on long-distance radio transmission, and the development of Marconi's law and radio telegraph system. He is credited as the inventor of radio and he shared the 1909 Nobel Prize in Physics with Karl Ferdinand Braun "in recognition of their contributions to the development of wireless telegraphy".

3 Marconi made the announcement that the message was received using a 500 foot (150 metre) kite-supported antenna for reception signals transmitted by the Marconi Company's

new high-power station based at Poldhu; the distance between the two points was approximately 2,200 miles (3,500 kilometres).

4 Louis Charles Joseph Blériot (1872-1936) was a French aviator, inventor, and engineer. He was also the first to make a working, powered, piloted monoplane. In July 1909 he became world-famous for making the first airplane flight across the English Channel winning the prize of £1,000 offered by the *Daily Mail* newspaper.

5 When the *Titanic* struck an iceberg and sank on 14th April 1912, the 712 survivors owed their lives to the distress calls from the Marconi wireless equipment on board. As Lord Samuel, Postmaster General at the time stated: "Those who have been saved have been saved through one man, Mr. Marconi and his wonderful invention."

6 On 2nd April 1908, the 380-ton destroyer *HMS Tiger* took part in a Home Fleet exercise 20 miles south of the Isle of Wight to test defences against torpedo boats. Built in 1900 for the Admiralty by John Brown and Co, Clydebank she had a speed of 30 knots and was armed with one 12-pounder and two torpedo tubes. During the exercise, *HMS Tiger* crossed the bow of a nearby cruiser, *HMS Berwick*, and was sliced in half, her bow section sinking almost immediately. Fortunately, the stern section stayed afloat long enough for most of her 63 crew to be rescued, but the captain and 27 members of the crew were drowned.

7 *HMS Gladiator* was a second class protected cruiser of the Royal Navy, launched on 8 December 1896 at Portsmouth, England. During a late snowstorm off the Isle of Wight on 25th April 1908, *Gladiator* was heading into port when she struck the outbound American steamer SS *Saint Paul*. A total of 27 sailors were lost, but only three bodies were recovered.

8 Golden Hill Fort was a defensible barracks at Freshwater, Isle of Wight built as part of the Palmerston defences by the 1859 Royal Commission on the Defence of the United Kingdom to provide manpower for the defences at the western end of the Isle of Wight. Built in hexagonal form, it accommodated eight officers and 128 men and had its own hospital.

Isle of Wight Constabulary, 1907.
William is in the back row, second left.
Chief Constable Isle of Wight Constabulary Captain Harry
George Adams-Connor is seated front row, far left.
© Hampshire Constabulary History Society.

(right) Examples of the birch used for
criminal and corporal punishment.
@ National Archives.

5

CRIME AND PUNISHMENT

In the days of my Father's police career there were no juvenile courts but the birch was used regularly, a system of punishment that inflicted great pain and suffering from which one did not easily recover. As a dedicated Policeman he never agreed to this form of punishment, his view was with parents being firm and the local Police being tough, many would be law-abiding. He hated cruelty and neglect of children and had many cases during his career. Arguably the hardest part of a Constable's job is dealing with children's misfortune.

On many occasions Mother took children into our home to wash and feed, preparing them to go to the only outcome left to them – the workhouse. Very little compassion was afforded such children and I remember the numerous times a child was taken with the horse-drawn carriage to the workhouse. The cries and screams of those poor mites stayed with Father for he knew how hard life would be for them. Once they arrived at the workhouse he escorted them inside frequently met by a very cold and bitter woman. It's a side of Policing he hated.

In March 1906 he was involved in an incident whilst on duty at a parish council election where he had been since 8.00 a.m. On the way home after his usual 12 hours of duty he stopped to chat with the local postmaster at his house and before long, he was called by a man who was a servant of Farringford House, the home of Lord Tennyson the poet. He reported that a man had broken into the stables and was causing havoc. Straightway Father attended the site and caught the man who appeared to be very drunk. Thinking the best plan would be to escort the man home rather than the cells they began walking towards his house. It was a dark, cold night and as they approached an alley the man produced a sharp bladed knife and attempted to stab my Father in the chest. Thank-

old but I can remember those drive
today I often compare the things
for children's welfare with those
when no kind word was given to
these children when they arrived at
Workhouse. They were received generally
a Hard faced woman to whom it w
just another job and whished away
even allowing us to say goodbye. I
was only just one side of the Villa
policeman's duty. Another incident
affected him personally occurred
March 1906. There had been an
Election for the Parish Council and m
father had been on duty all day fr
8 a m till after the election
declaration of the poll and wa
returning home very tired w

*Extract from Ellen Foyle's original
"Memories of My Father 1867-1951".
© JH Greenfield Family Settlement.*

fully, his quick reactions saved his life but not before the man had stabbed his hand. Drawing his truncheon and raising alarm with his whistle – quickly responded to by a soldier – the man was over-powered and placed under arrest. They were assisted to Yarmouth Police station where Father's hand was stitched up and the man placed into the cell.

When the case came before the court Father stood in the dock and made a request to the judge that the charge be reduced to common assault. How or why he would do this angered many. To this day I do not know the reason for such an action on his part but the judge residing heard his plea and reluctantly agreed. Even with a reduced charge the man received a sentence of two years because judges took a very serious view of injuring Police Constables.

Three years later Father was on duty in Newport when a very smartly dressed man approached him. It was the very same drunken man, George King, who had stabbed him and been to prison. He told Father he had never been in trouble before and felt remorse for his drunken actions and thanked him for his kindness in helping reduce the charge. He continued by saying due to Father's quick actions in over-powering his stupid drunken behaviour he lived to tell the story and served only 30 months of hard labour. Father's response to George's words was one of pleasure that he was remorseful and that life had taken a different path. We often spoke of this incident for my Father's actions and conduct had indeed changed a man's life. As his daughter I never questioned his actions or decisions again.

There was another very bad case, that of a soldier, a Major who had served I believe in the Boer War and was said to be quite a good shot. Apparently when practising his shooting at Ventnor he went

Sketch of Lord Tennyson sitting in his arbour at Farrinford House, Freshwater, 1892. Published in Appleton's Annual Cyclopaedia and Register of Important Events, 1893.

to the target to view his accuracy and slipped on some brick steps. The pistol he was holding discharged and he was hit by a bullet in the chest. Father said that the shot actually hit his heart and regrettably the Major passed away. He was only 38 at the time of this tragic event. Guns can protect us but they are dangerous even in trained hands as this calamitous accident showed.

I recall yet another incident, one of the most sorrowful my Father handled and that too involved a soldier who in this particular instance killed his wife and then himself. This happened at Brading [1] and he was found lying dead in his scullery with horrific injuries to his head. On investigating further Father discovered the wife dead from gunshots to her head in the stable. I can still picture how upset he was while telling my Mother of this tragic event. It seemed the soldier had suffered terrible and profound distress and his mind was affected greatly. Local enquiries showed that he had been in hospital and was placed on leave pending removal from service. The case was placed before the coroner who subsequently found that the soldier killed his wife and himself whilst being of unsound mind. It's not easy for me to write about this case more openly as it was dreadful but it demonstrates how hurt a person's mind can become.

* * *

I wish to elaborate a little now on the man behind the Police uniform. After Father's arrival at Freshwater there were additions to our family making seven in all, three more sons and a daughter, William, Christopher, Jack and Ada. His career had taught us to be respectful and appreciate what little we had. It was a hard struggle to raise a large family even though we had a home and Father received a regular wage. Times were tough. Police Constables earned five gold sovereigns and although Father earned slightly more the difference was taken as rent for our Police house. It was hard for a large family such as ours but with him being a well-liked local Constable quite often a sack of potatoes and bags of vegetables would mysteriously arrive on our doorstep. Our family never wanted for food and it was his wish that if we could help the less fortunate by sharing ours we should. We were clothed and dressed properly and his Police colleagues would often tell us how smart we looked. Mother was good at making and mending so we always had clothes with no holes.

While Father cared passionately about his career his family were the most important part of his life. He planted every inch of our garden with vegetables often sharing the produce with his colleagues.

William in uniform, 1907.
© *Hampshire Constabulary History Society.*

He mended all our shoes and boots and helped Mother in the house when his duty allowed. I could write so much about how he did everything within his power to make our lives as good as we had. I would ask why he was like this to which he usually replied, "I care about life, I care about people be it my family or others." I can tell you it was his Policing career that made him this way. To have discipline, compassion, honour, dignity; I am so proud his life took him down the path of being a Police Constable.

Freshwater being a military area meant his workload was very busy and because of the increasing numbers of people who came from outside the area it also attracted some of the worst types. As a result two more Constables were brought across, one stationed at Freshwater and the other at Totland Bay. This gave him extra help and in coming months proved to be a wise move by the Isle of Wight Constabulary. Often there would be altercations at the military base, which he investigated, for even though soldiers, at times they fought one another.

Then came the day he was promoted to Sergeant, for although special it was tinged with sadness for it meant we had to move from Freshwater back to Newport. The local community raised a petition asking if my newly promoted Father could remain at Freshwater. It was declined. The rules were the rules and you had to abide by the senior officer's authority. This was followed up by a further request from the community who wished to recognise his outstanding service with a presentation, this too was disallowed. It didn't seem right to us that being so well-liked and respected meant having to relocate.

Notes

1 Brading is located on the east side of the Isle of Wight, a short distance from Ryde, and is one of its oldest towns that many years ago formed a major port before the area was fully reclaimed in the late nineteenth century.

Isle of Wight Constabulary helmet plate, c.1890.
*© https://en.wikipedia.org/wiki/Isle_of_*
Wight_Constabulary

The High Street, Newport.
Engraved by George Bannon, 1831.

6

BACK TO NEWPORT

Once again we moved back to Newport. For us children it was a huge change and certainly a new way of life as we moved to a town where the lights, shops and street traders felt like a whole new world. Two of my brothers left school and started to earn a wage which helped. A new chapter in Father's Policing career began. His duties changed, we had more regular family time and could plan days unlike before. While at Newport he dealt with many cases and one in particular I will mention.

This was a case of arson and a young engaged couple were the offenders. The woman concerned was the proprietor of a small fancy and general goods shop in Fairlee Road. She was a few years older than her fiancé and very keen to get wed. The business was not doing well and bills were mounting although it was well covered by insurance. Her fiancé was not employed in the shop and was out of work. One day passing the door whilst on his beat Father noticed smoke coming from under the front door. On checking he found the door locked but the shop inside on fire. Upon blowing his whistle he was assisted by others who forced entry to the shop to find the carpets ablaze. Upon further investigation they found more goods on fire with the Fire Brigade shortly arriving having a station nearby. The fire was put out and circumstances pointed to arson.

Enquires were made and subsequently the couple arrested and charged with arson. Due to the nature of this crime the case was heard at Winchester Assizes where the judge gave the man 18 months hard labour and the woman a two-year suspended sentence. She did not go to prison but served her sentence on what was called probation and involved undertaking good works to help others. The judge passed light sentences as he was aware of the previous good character of both. I recall when the man was eventually released the couple were asked to leave the Island and did so.

There was very little mercy for prisoners and those who broke the law were punished no matter what their crime. For the law is what must be obeyed by all who wish to live in our wonderful country. Prison life was very hard, some much harder than others especially if sentenced to hard labour. However, "trusted prisoners" were given tasks of work to undertake with the intention of helping them understand how breaking the law

*A prisoner forced to turn a crank handle repeatedly
as a form of punishment, 1884.
© Old Prison Cells Museum.*

Newport Prison.

was the wrong action. One such task I remember Father recounting was that of shoemaker; it was also when tools were given to trusted prisoners. An incident happened one cold winter's day at Newport Prison, where many people who committed terrible crimes were sent to serve long sentences. On this particular occasion a young man used his hammer to attack a fellow prisoner and injure the warder who was overseeing the shoe-making in the work area.

As in most instances such as this the local Constable had to attend and oversee what action needed to be undertaken. On arriving at the prison Father was informed of the incident and because the young man was of unsound mind he had been placed in a prison cell on his own – I think this was called solitary punishment. Sadly, the man he had hurt was very badly injured and taken by Father and a warder to the local hospital where his wounds were treated. He never recovered. A prison Doctor described the injuries to Father and so serious were they the man had lost his ability to talk and walk and could therefore only be cared for by doctors and nurses. The case of a further sentence was presented to the judge but we never found out what happened to the man who committed this terrible act.

Such was a Constable's life in the early 1900s and for this reason it was important to take each day at a time for they never knew what would happen once they went on the beat. We were always scared Father would be hurt or even worse and many times he said to us, "We are Police Constables and the town's folk know to behave when we are around." Not everyone did I learnt and as I wrote many times in my diaries over the years our Constables had a lot of support from the judges should someone cross the line of the law.

Whipping post, 1895.
© National Archives.

As the weeks and months went by I heard of many more crimes. It seems to me that people who have nothing try hard but they fall and this makes them take from those who have more, bringing me to the young boy just nine years old who Father encountered one cold December night. A local store-keeper had reported that the young child had taken a few potatoes and run off towards the woods. Following the way the boy had run Father caught him huddling and shaking, crying in a leaky cold horse cart that had been abandoned with one wheel. Being the man he was, he took off his Police overcoat and wrapped the poor boy in it to keep him warm for December nights on the Isle of Wight get cold with a bitter wind or snow that comes across the sea. He was very unwell and Father knew he had a serious illness. Carrying him home to our Police house, cold and shaking he arrived late into the night. We made the poor boy a bed beside our fire to warm him and after some time he was able to tell us that his Mother was asleep at the back of the store from where he had stolen the potatoes. He also said his name was Archibald James. Father instinctively knew this was not good and went back out to investigate. Upon returning it was indeed a very tragic story unfolding. In fact, the boy's Mother had passed away while working in the backyard of the store. Archibald had tried to wake her as he was hungry. Unable to do so took it upon himself to find something to eat. I write this day in my diaries with tears flowing for Father had to tell the poor boy his Mother had gone to heaven and I can still picture him holding the boy in his arms as he cried and screamed, still shaking with his illness.

When daylight came I went to get the local Doctor who quickly came round to our Police house. Whilst he was attending the boy, Father returned to the store and oversaw the undertakers, two brothers by the name of Weaver who were well-known in Newport and were removing the body. My parents decided Archibald must rest and get well for the Doctor had diagnosed an illness of the chest. Getting permission from his Inspector, Father and Mother continued to help the boy recover from his illness. After two weeks or so he was considerably better, alas his future as in many cases such as this was within the workhouse. I cried the day he left as did my Mother for we knew this poor lad would have much to deal with, but would at least have food and a place to sleep.[1]

Life went on day-to-day, we were very grateful for what we had and it was so important that we give thanks for this. The Sunday after we had taken

87

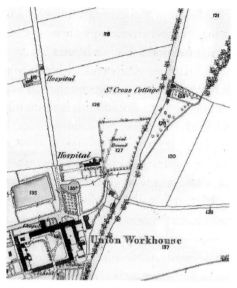

Newport House of Industry – "The Grubber".
© *http://www.workhouses.org.uk/IsleOfWight*

Archibald James to the workhouse we all went to
our local church. Father spoke to the chaplain and
told him about Archibald and during our prayers
he asked God to grant this poor boy some peace
in life. My wish is that our Lord granted this for
from that day onward as we never knew what
happened to Archibald.

The weeks and months slipped by and our days
were happy most of the time. The family was
growing, Father had established himself once

88

again as the local Police Sergeant and life was improving. The local residents were very accepting of his strict methods. The ale houses got to know him as did street vendors and all kinds of other folk in Newport. He was strict but he was fair and as the weeks passed life became a little easier.

The Isle of Wight at this time had very little industry but I was now old enough to work as was my brother Stanley and my sister Alice, and so we were able and happy to contribute to the family home. Although we were not wealthy our joint incomes helped make our lives more pleasant.

The first break in our family came when Stanley reached 18 and he took the "Queen's Shilling", a well-known term used when joining the Army. My Father was very proud, my Mother heartbroken, with our lives suddenly changing as she became ill as a result of Stanley completing his training and posted overseas. Home life was difficult some days with my parents disagreeing on matters. The years were going by and he had given long service of 26 years and was considering his future because of Mother's health and with her hair turning white with worry. More and more he was working very long hours, his role as a Sergeant meant he had authority over other Constables. In spite of his rank they were very fond of him because although tough he was fair. He was doing well, again lots of arrests, some awful cases before the courts until one day in October 1912 when a messenger came to the station with a hand-written letter. Upon opening it Father was shocked to read he had been placed forward for promotion and was formally summoned before the Chief Constable, Captain Harry Adams-Connor.[2]

At this meeting he was offered the position of Inspector and to continue his work upon his beloved Island, ultimately entailing a lot more work and likely more hours. The role would involve the oversight of numerous matters, control and discipline of lower ranks, and stopping pay or pensions for those not complying with duty rules. Humbled by this great offer of promotion he asked for time to consider the new position. He had to think about the implications of the promotion and spent several days deep in thought troubled by the outcome of whatever his decision might be and took long walks to think over his plan. After all he had done, the hard work, the long hours of dedication to duty, all this played upon his mind profoundly, and yet one aspect troubled him the most – how his career was now affecting his beloved family.

Finally, he made his decision to put us first and with much sadness tendered his resignation to the Chief Constable, a man of great honour and someone

Chief Constable Isle of Wight Constabulary,
Captain Harry George Adams-Connor, May 1927.
Photographer, Lafayette. ©National Portrait Gallery.

many knew and respected. Father explained why he had to put his family before his duties and spoke openly with the Chief Constable about his feelings and passion for the job he loved. He felt terrible sadness at this decision but he had given so much and his family were affected. The Chief Constable understood and accepted with equal sadness the loss of a highly regarded Police Sargent.

Within a short period of time we saw our final Christmas on the Island. A time when we all reflected on our adventures, one of sorrow too for we knew our hearts dwelt upon the Isle of Wight. Our Christmas was one of joy and thanks for what we had but we knew it would be so very troubling leaving the Island for the last time. As always Father explained why in life things do not last forever and we understood. To this day, I remember standing in our garden with the snow falling upon me, looking around knowing this would be our final goodbye. I cried, not ashamed to relate this for I loved our Police house, our garden, and the friendships we had made. The thoughts of this being no longer part of our daily lives hurt deep inside.

Our belongings were packaged up through January and our Police house was passed to another Constable. Thus, with heavy hearts and crying tears we left our beloved Isle of White on 31st January 1913 and relocated to Southampton. We took residence at a house in Netley alongside the shoreline, new beginnings for us all, worried days ahead for we needed work and regular income.

Notes

1 In 1774 the second workhouse in Britain was founded in Newport on the Isle of Wight – The Isle of Wight House of Industry – later from 1902 known as Forest House, although popularly nicknamed "The Grubber". The elderly, infirm and disabled, the unemployed, widows, unmarried parents, their illegitimate children, orphans and the young were incarcerated within its walls in conditions similar to those found within gaols, with the stigmatized inmates treated worse than slaves. The workhouse system was designed to look at each person as a cost-cutting exercise. It wasn't until 1930 that "The Grubber" was officially dissolved, although many would continue to live there. Today the buildings are offices and meeting rooms for St Mary's Hospital and are Grade II Listed.

2 Captain Harry George Adams-Connor C.V.O., D.L. (1859-1939) was Chief Constable from 1899 until 1935. He was a twin son of the Very Rev. George H. Connor, the first vicar of Newport, and afterwards Dean of Windsor and chaplain to Queen Victoria. He served for 20 years in the Connaught Rangers seeing active service in the Boar War of 1880-81.

Royal Victoria Military Hospital, Netley, Hampshire
during First World War.
© Hampshire County Archives.

7

SOUTHAMPTON, THE WHITE STAR LINE AND ROYAL VICTORIA MILITARY HOSPITAL, NETLEY

It was not long before Father had found suitable work that he had seen advertised in a local store. Once more taking his courage and bringing his previous training to the fore he applied to the White Star Shipping Line [1] based in Southampton Docks. With his Police record as a man of honour he became Master-at-Arms for the new shipping line, an excellent job with good wages.

Finally, Mother's health improved and family life began to settle but Father was missing his role as a Police Sargeant. He often talked to her about the decision he had taken and I fear he felt much unhappiness on many occasions. His passion and his love of people and the Isle of Wight never left his mind. My brother Stanley was serving in Malta

SS Homeric, White Star Dock, 1911.
© *https://www.shippingwondersoftheworld.com*

by now and although we received letters from him my parents barely let a day go by without saying a prayer for his safe return.

Then suddenly the talk of war was thrust upon us even while we hoped it would never come. On 4th August 1914 the blow came and Great Britain was at war with Germany.

The war brought significant change, family life was harder, nerves were stretched and people worried constantly about loved ones. The day soon arrived when the military took over Southampton Docks and within a short time all of the non-military shipping and business in the docks was relocated to Liverpool which meant Father had to go also if he wanted to keep his job.[2] Once more his life's path had placed an obstacle in his way. He declined to go and was left unemployed but not for long for he had a family and this was his purpose. His life to date had shown that problems can be overcome if you are positive. Therefore when he saw a job advertised for a Police Constable at the Royal Victoria Military Hospital he felt it was a way to become once more a Police Constable.

The Royal Victoria Military Hospital[3] on the shore of Southampton Water was a magnificent building with vast corridors and a chapel. The view over Southampton Water from Netley where we lived reminded Father of his life up to that point, the Island and the docks. Before long and after a short process he became the Hospital's Police Constable and was back in uniform. This marked the start of a second Police career, one that meant overseeing thousands of patients during the war years, listening to terrible stories of suffering, and dealing with soldiers with severe injuries. [4] He found it hard to witness his fellow man so badly hurt. One thing he was especially troubled by was tucked away out of sight – this was D-Block – the first purpose-built military asylum. It was here that the fate of soldiers suffering with mental issues from what they had seen in battle were kept, and it fell upon others to decide if they would either be going home, sent to a lunatic asylum or posted back to the front line. From a Policing view most of the incidents he dealt with were sadly those relating to the patients in D-Block.

The hospital complex included officers' quarters, a railway station and stables. It also had its own dedicated pier which many people wandered along. During Father's service at the Royal Victoria the war poet Wilfred Owen [5] was a patient having been injured in action. He had been hit by the explosion of a shell when serving on the front line in 1917 and his brief stay at Netley saw him assessed for shell shock. Father would tell me of the many days he would hear screams and cries from D-Block, an experience with which he had to come to terms. [6] It's hard to imagine what some of these soldiers had witnessed and what terrible images lay in their minds.

By the time Armistice came ending the Great War he was now 51 years old, in good health and still working at the hospital.

*Amputee serviceman at Royal Victoria
Military Hospital. © National Archives.*

*Shell-shocked patient at Royal Victoria Military Hospital.
© British Pathé.*

Notes

1 The Oceanic Steam Navigation Company, more commonly known as the White Star Line (WSL) was a British shipping company. Founded out of the remains of a defunct packet company, it gradually rose up as one of the most prominent shipping lines in the world, providing passenger and cargo services between the British Empire and the United States.

2 During the First World War Southampton Docks became the number one military embarkation port for troops leaving for the war in France. It was "Port Number One" for sending soldiers to the Front. *Southampton Port, Hampshire: Gateway to the War,* https://www.bbc.co.uk/programmes/p022y9c0, BBC broadcast, April 2014.

3 Britain's first purpose-built military hospital opened in 1863. Grand in scale, the Royal Victoria Military Hospital on the waterfront at Netley in Hampshire had its own railway station and 1,000 beds. A corridor stretched for a quarter of a mile from one end of the hospital to the other and during the First World War the wards overflowed with wounded soldiers. As early as 1914, the 200-acre grounds were beginning to fill up with huts to treat vast numbers of casualties. This extension was managed by the Red Cross. The ferocity of the fighting brought its own medical challenges. Netley doctors amputated limbs and refined blood transfusions. Mustard gas victims were treated in special saline baths. A contemporaneous film made in 1917 entitled *War Neuroses* depicts attempts to "cure" shell-shock, although some of the footage has now been shown to be faked. See *Royal Victoria Country Park, Hampshire: Palace for Broken Men*, BBC radio broadcast, https://www.bbc.co.uk/sounds/play/p01yn7hp

4 When Arthur Conan Doyle published his first Sherlock Holmes mystery, *A Study in Scarlet*, he told his readers that

Dr Watson trained as an army doctor at Netley – its name was so well known that the author had no need to explain any further.

5 Wilfred Edward Salter Owen, MC (1893-1918) was an English poet and soldier. He was one of the leading poets of the First World War. He was killed in action on 4th November 1918 during the crossing of the Sambre–Oise Canal exactly one week (almost to the hour) before the signing of the Armistice which ended the war.

6 *Inside the Royal Victoria Hospital*, BBC broadcast, 28th May 2014. https://www.bbc.co.uk/programmes/p01zx2j9 See also Hoare, Philip, *Spike Island. The Memory of a Military Hospital*, Fourth Estate, 2010, and Hoare, Philip, "Palace of pain: Netley, the hospital built for an empire of soldiers", *Guardian*, 21st August 2014.

William and his wife Ellen, 1945.
© JH Greenfield Family Settlement.

8

POST-WAR, RETIREMENT, MORE WAR AND LIFE BEYOND 70

Father would often say how proud he was of his family and how we had remained happy even in difficult times. His Policing career took him into his 70s, and he and Mother had kept in good health continuing to enjoy many years of happily married life. Nonetheless, at the age of 72 he decided to make a change by moving back to Stockbridge – where he first met my mother – handing his resignation in at the Royal Victoria. In 1939 and within less than two decades the Second World War broke out and they both felt that distancing themselves from the war, the noise and its preparations would help them now they were in retirement. Family life would continue as best it could though living daily through the years of yet another war was taxing. Being ex-Police

Father undertook being a fire watcher, a task Mother was very nervous about as bombs would drop from the sky with the siren not always being heard.

He also became a parish councillor and Mother helped in nursing and with both being in their mid-70s this was some achievement. Unfortunately, this was not to last for without warning Mother took ill with a haemorrhage in the head. Recovering slowly but with limited abilities they continued to take each day at a time. On 20th November 1946 we celebrated Mother's 76th birthday with a family gathering at their home in Stockbridge. It was a wonderful day with everyone enjoying the precious moments and all returned home that night believing she was doing well. For the next few months they spent time relaxing and reminiscing as best they could, her ability to remember was not as it had once been. Then without warning on 30th November 1947 the call came that Father had tried to get help for but her long life was over. His beloved wife Ellen had passed away in her sleep. Father was devastated and his heart was broken, so many memories, so much done and achieved as husband and wife. Our family had lost its first link. Having lost his partner of 56 years of married life we decided as a family that Father must be our first priority.

We brought Mother back to Netley as it was her wish to be laid to rest in the local church-yard at Hound Cemetery and were left to carry on without her presence and devoted love. Father relocated to my sister Gwen's house in Hamble and it was here he lived out his final years. As you might expect he missed Mother greatly for his love was with him no more. He would take many visits to the church-yard and stand by her grave talking to her. Love has no boundaries and

William with his grandson Graham,
Hamble, 1948.
© JH Greenfield Family Settlement.

he knew one day they would be together again. He attended the local church in Hamble and continued steadfastly to give thanks for the life he had lived and the path he had taken. The family spent as much time as we could with him and Gwen cared for him very well. He kept healthy and not once did he lose sight of his passion, that of his Police career, and would tell many stories of that life often repeating them over and over to our amusement.

Hamble was close to the water, the beach was somewhere Father would go for walks. It was a very stony beach and one with much shelter from trees and growth. He spent many a-day walking there and looking across the sea to the Isle of Wight where he had spent so many happy years. He was a proud Police Sargent one who had devoted most of his adult life to helping others and he never forgot this. His recollections of events, his love of the Police, my Mother and the life they shared were never far from his thoughts.

And now my tears flow writing this final piece. A day in my life I shall never forget until I am in his safe care. My sister had called Father for dinner after he had gone upstairs to sleep. She found that his wish to be reunited with Mother had been granted and so it was on 3rd February 1951 William Foyle passed from our world. After many years together and a short time apart my beloved parents were reunited into God's safekeeping.

William and Ellen Foyle may have departed from us but the life we shared with our parents will be with us in our hearts until we all meet again and become one family in heaven. The story I have shared here will, I hope, make interesting reading in years to come. My diaries on which this account is based are filled with many stories about life with a Father in such a wonderful job. A Police Constable who rose to the rank of Sargeant with an abiding passion to help the many not the few. He was a truly great, honourable man who did both his Constabularies proud. While some of what I recount is immensely sad other recollections are happier but this was our family life in England from the 1890s to the early decades of the unfolding twentieth century. A country my dear Father loved and gave of his life's energy to ensure the laws were upheld.

I could have written many reams
of incidents of his life but
illness prevents me. — enough
has been written which may
interest his grandchildren and
great grandchildren to know
that if they follow his
example in their lives
they will never regret being
members of the
family bearing the
name of "Foyle" for it is a good
one.

E. R. Thompson
(daughter)

Original extract from Ellen Foyle's
"Memories of My Father 1867-1951"
© JH Greenfield Family Settlement.

Ellen Thompson née Foyle, 1958.
© JH Greenfield Family Settlement.

108

MY CLOSING THOUGHTS ...

Father lies with Mother at rest in the church-yard at Hound Cemetery in Netley. I could have written reams of stories and incidents in his life. A man who gave to others more than he ever took. A man of courage and great honour, and a man who wore his Police uniform with enormous pride. Enough is written here to be passed to family and friends in years to come so they too can discover a Police Constable's lot can be a happy and fulfilled one. Devotion to duty, caring for your fellow man makes a difference in this world. Father proved that this attitude works and it is my wish as his daughter Ellen Foyle that those who read this account know the name of Foyle is stamped irrevocably into Policing history.

ACKNOWLEDGEMENTS

This book embodies a multi-generational family endeavour spanning 153 years during which the Boer War and two World Wars raged, women campaigned and achieved the vote, the Welfare State and the NHS were created, the British Empire took its final bow, and a second Elizabethan age flourished.

Whilst many people have encouraged and inspired me over the evolution of this book and to whom I am very grateful, there are those who deserve especial recognition.

First, has to be my grandmother Ellen Thompson née Foyle who kept, annotated, and melded William's original diaries with her own recollections of his life and that of their policing family from the late Victorian age to 1951. It was from her memoir that I have based *So You Want To Be A Peeler, Eh Boy?*, thereby ensuring their collective experience is not lost to future generations of my extended family but also to officers and members of the UK Police Constabularies.

My own mother – and Ellen's daughter – Margaret Greenfield has played a significant role as it was she, who first told me of Ellen's memoirs, and kindly gave me this precious family inheritance to safeguard and then, to ensure its publication.

There's a great deal documented in my great grandfather William's story which reveals similarities between his and my own devotion to Policing. With this in mind I want to mention two Constabularies for whom I have worked, firstly Hampshire Constabulary and currently Dorset Constabulary. I would like to thank Simon Hayes, ex-Police Commissioner of Hampshire Constabulary for his wonderful contribution of the book's Foreword.

My thanks also extend to Derek Stevens, Secretary and Curator of the Hampshire Constabulary History Society, who kindly assisted in sourcing photographs of William in police uniform held in their archives at Solent Sky Museum, Southampton.

Credit should also go to my splendid friend and lawyer Sarah Dixon, who kindly set up the legal entities relating to our Family Trust.

None of what you read within these pages would have been as good without the invaluable expertise of Dr Susan England of Burnt Toast Editorial, whose guidance has helped me throughout.

On the creativity front has been the significant contribution of talented book designer Briony Hartley of Goldust Design, and Anthony Wakeford-Brown of Magic Box Media; his expertise on brand identity has been a key development for the book and future of Greenfield Productions Ltd.

I could not have undertaken this endeavour without the patience of my dear wife Sheila who has been my rock since the very first day our paths crossed. Her patience and understanding has been deeply loving and truly humbling.

My daughter Kirsty Stanley and her partner Matt deserve a special mention for their wholehearted support of my ambition to bring a wider readership to *So You Want To Be A Peeler, Eh Boy?*

I would like to doff my cap to Chris Greenfield, my dear son who is also my business partner and supporter of my passion for Policing.

And finally, all of my grandchildren: Emily, Vince, Charlie, Kyle, Kaycee, Sophia, and Coby.

John Greenfield

BIBLIOGRAPHY AND FURTHER READING

Primary sources
Official and archival records
England & Wales Marriage Index 1837-2000
England & Wales Census of 1861
England & Wales Census of 1871
England & Wales Census of 1881
England & Wales Census of 1911
Agricultural Labour Census of 1871
Hampshire County Council Archives
Hampshire Archives Trust
National Archives

Historical societies
Hampshire Constabulary History Society
Old Police Cells Museum

Historic Prints
Brannon, George, *Vectis scenery: being a series of original and select views exhibiting the picturesque beauties, local peculiarities and places of particular interest in the Isle of Wight drawn from nature.* 1831.

Online

http://www.workhouses.org.uk/Warminster/#Records

https://www.historic-uk.com/HistoryUK/Historyof
England/Sir-Robert-Peel

https://en.wikipedia.org/wiki/Robert_Peel

http://www.annbarrett.co.uk/police/police-snippets-
from-old-newspapers/

https://en.wikipedia.org/wiki/New_Zealand_Wars

http://www.chitterne.com/history/

http://www.ventnortowncouncil.org.uk/about-famous.php

https://www.reading.ac.uk/special-collections/
collections/sc-craigie.aspx

https://canadianbritishhomechildren.weebly.com/
indentured-servants.html

http://www.barrym0iow.co.uk/marconi/

http://woottonbridgeiow.org.uk/wibook/index.php

https://www.isle-of-wight-fhs.co.uk/index.php

https://en.wikipedia.org/wiki/Farringford_House

http://www.olioweb.me.uk/echoes/?page_id=240

https://undereveryleaf.wordpress.com/2017/09/17/
the-h-m-s-tiger-disaster-2nd-april-1908/

https://h2g2.com/entry/A87782638

https://en.wikipedia.org/wiki/Isle_of_Wight_
Constabulary

Television, radio and film

Southampton Port, Hampshire: Gateway to the War,
BBC broadcast, April 2014, https://www.bbc.co.uk/
programmes/p022y9c0

Inside the Royal Victoria Hospital, BBC broadcast, 28th
May 2014, https://www.bbc.co.uk/programmes/
p01zx2j9

Royal Victoria Country Park, Hampshire: Palace for Broken Men, BBC radio broadcast, https://www.bbc.co.uk/sounds/play/p01yn7hp

War Neuroses, (1917), British Pathé, https://www.youtube.com/watch?v=lrRU37beCJ4

Newspapers and journals
Hoare, Philip, "Palace of pain: Netley, the hospital built for an empire of soldiers", *Guardian*, 21st August 2014.

Secondary sources
Coe, Lewis, *Wireless Radio: A History*, (McFarland & Co), 2nd revised edition, 2006.

Hoare, Philip, *Spike Island. The Memory of a Military Hospital*, (Fourth Estate), 2010.

Lee, John, Penke, Colin, Stevens, Derek and Williams, Clifford, *Policing Hampshire and the Isle of Wight. A Photographic History*, (Phillimore & Co. Ltd), 2001.

Raboy, Marc, *The Man Who Networked the World*, (OUP), 2016.

Robinson, Sue, *Chitterne: A Wiltshire Village*, (Hobnob Press), 2007.

Watt, Ian A., *A History of the Hampshire and Isle of Wight Constabulary 1839-1966*, (Phillimore & Co. Ltd), second edition, 2006.

Weightman, Gavin, *Signor Marconi's Magic Box: The invention that sparked the radio revolution*, (Harper Collins), 2004.

ILLUSTRATIONS AND PHOTOGRAPHS

Figure photograph
William Foyle, 1907. (Hampshire Constabulary History Society).

Frontispieces
1. Extract from Ellen Foyle's original "Memories of My Father 1867–1951". (JH Greenfield Family Settlement)
2. Hampshire Constabulary officers who transferred to the Isle of Wight on 31 March 1890. (Hampshire Constabulary History Society).
3. *A New and Corrected Map of the Isle of Wight* and *Outline of the Southern Coast of England.* Engraved by George Bannon, 1831.
4. Marconi's Transmitter at Knowles Farm, Niton, adjacent to St Catherine's Point Lighthouse, Isle of Wight. (Isle of Wight History Society).
5. Isle of Wight Constabulary, 1907. (Hampshire Constabulary History Society)
6. Isle of Wight Constabulary helmet plate, c.1890. https://en.wikipedia.org/wiki/Isle_of_Wight_Constabulary
7. Royal Victoria Military Hospital, Netley, Hampshire

p.75 Sketch of Lord Tennyson sitting in his arbour at Farrinford House, Freshwater, 1892. https://en.wikipedia.org/wiki/Farringford_House

p.78 William in uniform, 1907. (Hampshire Constabulary History Society).

p.80 Isle of Wight Constabulary helmet plate, c.1890. © https://en.wikipedia.org/wiki/Isle_of_Wight_Constabulary

p.80 The High Street, Newport. Engraved by George Bannon, 1831.

p.83 A prisoner forced to turn a crank handle repeatedly as a form of punishment, 1884. (Old Prison Cells Museum).

p.83 Newport Prison.

p.85 Whipping post, 1895. (National Archives).

p.88 Newport House of Industry ("The Grubber"). http://www.workhouses.org.uk/IsleOfWight/

p.91 Chief Constable Isle of Wight Constabulary, Captain Harry George Adams-Connor, May 1927. Photographer, Lafayette. (National Portrait Gallery).

p.96 *SS Homeric*, White Star Dock, 1911. https://www.shippingwondersoftheworld.com/

p.99 Amputee serviceman at Royal Victoria Military Hospital. (National Archives).

p.99 Shell-shocked patient at Royal Victoria Military Hospital. (British Pathé).

p.105 William with his grandson Graham, Hamble, 1948. (JH Greenfield Family Settlement).

p.108 Original extract from Ellen Foyle's "Memories of My Father 1867–1951". (JH Greenfield Family Settlement).

p.108 Ellen Thompson née Foyle, 1958. (JH Greenfield Family Settlement).

FOYLES OF CHITTERNE

**Extract from Foyles of Chitterne based on
Roger Foyle's family history research**

John married Ellen Dowdell at Fisherton Delamare in 1867 and had seven children.

Ellen Dowdell was born in January 1846 at
South Newton, the illegitimate daughter of Thirsa
Dowdell. Thirsa married Ellen's presumed father
John Potter in 1847 and they produced a large
family. John was a Royal Marine from 1836 to
1846 and had been away fighting in the Maori
Wars in New Zealand.

Ellen died in 1879 from an abscess on the brain.
This condition may explain why Caroline was
born at the Warminster Union Workhouse which
had a hospital attached. The various birth certifi-
cates show a movement around the Wylye Valley
area, consistent with John's occupations, and the
use of Dowdell and Potter as Ellen's maiden names.

At the time of the 1881 census the family
appears to be living together at Norton Bavant

but in fact had already broken up. William was living with his grandmother Thirsa Potter in Fisherton Delamare and Caroline lived with her paternal grandparents Samuel and Elizabeth. Rosina's whereabouts are unknown at the time but the four other children were in the Warminster Union Workhouse and by early 1882 John had abandoned them entirely, had a price on his head and a police warrant for his apprehension. It has to be assumed that John could not cope with his young family after Ellen's death at just 33 and the Union Trust Minutes state that he was unemployed for some time. Rosina was 12 and Tom was just over three (the 1881 census was conducted on 3rd and 4th April).

Whatever happened in that short period broke up the family but by 1882 John had married (Johanna) Caroline Murrell and was living in Weybridge in Surrey where in 1883, a son John was born. Recent research has discovered that John and Caroline moved to Elgin in Scotland soon after and had three more children. The son John migrated to Sydney, Australia in 1920 with his family while his surviving siblings seem to have remained in Scotland.

Lucy and Louisa were sent to Canada as Home Children by the Church Emigration Society, a foster care system that provided domestic help for farmers and the like in countries including Canada and Australia. They embarked on the *SS Toronto* at Liverpool on 12th August 1887 and arrived in Quebec on 22nd August 1887. This scheme in various forms continued into the 1960s but by the late 1980s was the subject of legal and social investigation leading to compensation and support for the children and families involved.

Little is known of Rosina in this period but it is believed she also went to Canada, possibly as part of a "Brides for Canada" scheme. She was later joined by her sister Ellen, who had been working at Ventnor, Isle of Wight where Annie was also working. Rosina moved later to Vancouver and married Benjamin Royal Crowder. They had four children, all born in Manitoba. Rosina also cared for some of her sister Ellen's children when she died prematurely. Their families may live in British Columbia.

Tom became a soldier in England then went to Canada, first as a volunteer in the Canadian Expeditionary Force during the First World War where he served as Sergeant Major, then with his family as a mines inspector after 1918 at Cobalt. Stanley's situation in those years is unknown although he appears in the 1891 census as a boarder at Corsley where he was a carter. He was close to his older brother William, whose descendants lived on the Isle of Wight until recent times. Stanley's grandson with his young family emigrated to Melbourne, Australia in 1958 not realizing that their ancestors had preceded them by 110 years!

Caroline Ann or Annie, married Alfred Smith in 1893 at Ventnor, Isle of Wight and they had three children. Her descendants live in Belfast and in Hertfordshire.

Ellen Frances or Nellie as she was known apparently had a child before marrying Christopher James Mitchell. They had four children in all, all born at Winchester (Canada). They may have moved to Winnipeg, Manitoba.

Stanley George married Annie Jane Nokes on Christmas Day 1894 at Heytesbury in Wiltshire. He was in the Royal Engineers during the First World War. Stanley and Annie had six children, the first born at Heytesbury and the others at Wandsworth.

Louisa, (Emma sometimes used), married Robert Frederick Foster on 10th September 1895 at Gananoque (Ontario, Canada). They had five children.

Lucy was raped by a person at the place where she was indentured as a Home Child and had a son. She later married Lewis Justin Bull and they had four children but she died aged 23.

Thomas returned to Wiltshire and married Eva Bessie Nokes, the sister of Annie Jane at Warminster in 1900. Tom was a soldier and a hunt groom and he and Eva had seven children. After the deaths of four of their children in 1906-1907 due to illnesses at Sutton Veny they moved to Amesbury where their last two children were born. Tom returned to Canada with his family circa. 1918 as a mines inspector and died by drowning in Alberta in 1931.

The above is an abbreviated version of my own line of descent. I have a family tree that shows circa 300 people living in the UK, Canada, Australia and New Zealand.

© Roger Foyle, 2012. See also
http://www.chitterne.com/history/foyles.html

JH GREENFIELD
FAMILY SETTLEMENT

The Greenfield family have long been aware of the existence of the policing memorabilia kept in an elderly relative's loft. When it was re-examined recently with a fresh perspective by John Greenfield it quickly became very apparent this was not just a sentimental collection kept for the family's sole enjoyment and reminiscence. It was so much more.

Instead, its value lies in the historical and auto-biographical record it provides of the fascinating realm of policing, police methods, crime and punishment, and its intersection with the rapidly changing social fabric of the late nineteenth and early twentieth centuries, nationally and communally. As a result of this new insight a decision was made by the family to ensure the collection is preserved for future generations.

Whilst the collection of diaries, images, letters, and many other policing items is very dear to the family it does not have a particular monetary value. Various legal mechanisms to best protect and preserve the integrity of the collection were discussed with the result of the creation of a Trust: the JH Greenfield Family Settlement.

Under this entity the family will retain all of the items under one legal entity. The Trust will own the physical items and all Intellectual Property Rights vested in them. As there may be interest from museums, libraries, historians, producers, dramatists, writers, and other parties in the collection, the Trustees are able to agree to loaning or licensing any part or parts of it, which will ensure that the collection will be protected at all times but also available to those who are interested in it.